Short Stack Editions | Volume 20

Rhubarb
by Sheri Castle

Short Stack Editions

Publisher: Nick Fauchald
Creative Director: Rotem Raffe
Editor: Kaitlyn Goalen
Copy Editor: Abby Tannenbaum
Marketing Manager: Erin Fritch

Text and recipes copyright © 2016 Sheri Castle.
Design and illustrations copyright © 2016 Rotem Raffe.
All rights reserved to Short Stack Editions.
Distributed in the United States by Dovetail Press (dovetail.press).
No portion of this book may be used or reproduced in any manner
whatsoever without written permission of the publisher.

ISBN 978-0-9907853-9-2

Printed in Virginia
Second printing, July 2017

Table of Contents

From the Editors	5
Introduction	7

Sweet

Rhubarb Pancakes with Rhubarb Syrup	10
Rhubarb Syrup	11
Roasted Rhubarb & Rosy Custard Trifle	12
Rhubarb Crumb Cake	14
Classic Rhubarb Jam	16
Sour Cream Rhubarb Pie with Ginger-Pecan Streusel	18

Savory

Fish Tacos with Rhubarb-Pineapple Salsa	20
Pulled Chicken Sandwiches with Rhubarb Barbecue Sauce	22
Rhubarb Barbecue Sauce	23
Smothered Chicken with Rhubarb Gravy	24
Rhubarb & Root Vegetable Tagine with Pistachio Couscous	26
Pecan-Crusted Salmon with Crisp Rhubarb & Apple Slaw	28
Old Fashioned Meatloaf with Rhubarb Ketchup	30
Rhubarb Ketchup	31

Pork Chops with Rhubarb Pan Dressing	33
Duck à la Rouge	34
Rhubarb & Tomato Dumplings	37
Rhubarb & Chard Gratin	38

Liquid

Herbed Rhubarb Lemonade	40
Tart Rhubarb Vinegar	41
Rhubarb Shrub (Shrubarb!)	42
Rhubarb Shrub Granita	43
Rhubarb Shrub Vinaigrette	43
Thank You!	45
Colophon	47

Without question, we publish each edition of Short Stack as its own unique cookbook that can function independently from the series. The edition that you hold in your hands, a love letter to rhubarb by an author whose devotion to the plant is in her genes, is no different: Sheri Castle's recipes speak to her personal connection to rhubarb and her own approachable ways to access it in the kitchen.

However, as we publish our 20th book under this project, we've realized that Short Stack, taken as a series, has morphed into an index, reminding us to revisit not only the familiar ingredients in our wheelhouse, but also those that we might not have ever reached for without the excuse of a pretty booklet. The lineup offers a push-pull for us as cooks; pushing us out of our comfort zone with one recipe, then pulling us back into the familiar and nostalgic with another.

Which brings us back to rhubarb. Beyond the populist rhubarb pie, the red-green ombré stalks got little play in our kitchen. We'd occasionally throw them into jams or pastries, sure, but couldn't really fathom their range of savory applications. Rhubarb is naturally acidic, a taste we depend on in keeping our cooking balanced. Thanks to this collection of recipes, we now think of rhubarb within the same hard-working family of lemons and vinegar—that is to say, it's become more of a staple than we'd ever have predicted.

If this is your first edition of Short Stack, welcome to the fold! If this is your 20th, here's to venturing outside of your comfort zone. We hope the adventure has been as eye-opening for you as it's been for us.

—*The Editors*

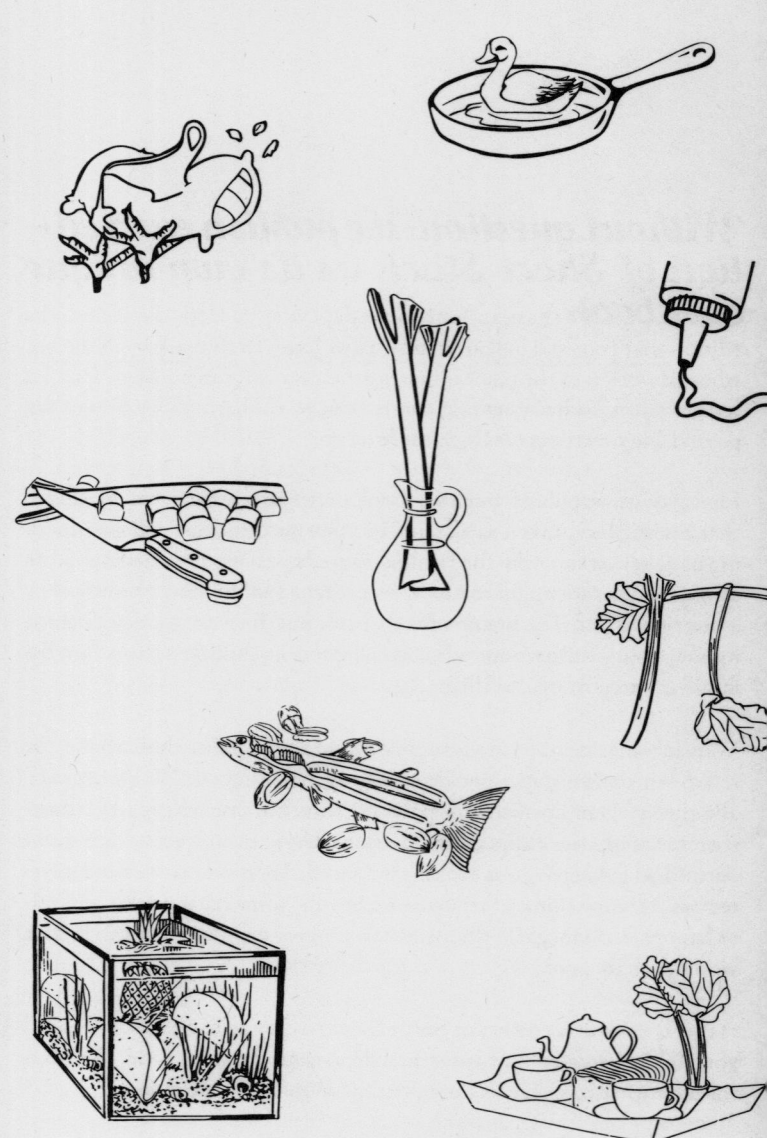

Introduction

I've had a crush on rhubarb my entire life. As a child, it was a snack that I could procure without the help of adults. I would go to the rhubarb patch that grew along the back edge of my grandparents' enormous garden, snap off a stalk and munch away. I sometimes carried a small cup of sugar or Tang mix that I would dip the stalks into; the sweetness would take a little of the sour edge away. Apparently, fondness for raw rhubarb runs through the Castle bloodline. My beloved grandmother Madge Reece Castle craved it throughout her three pregnancies. She'd waddle out to the garden with a salt shaker, generously season the raw stalks and eat her fill. And we all turned out just fine.

Rhubarb is a member of the buckwheat family and a close relative of sorrel, which might explain why it's so pleasingly acidic. It doesn't back down or get lost in recipes; it's bold and edgy. Pie remains the most common destination for rhubarb, so much so that some older cookbooks and garden logs called it "pie plant." But it's more versatile than you might think and can behave differently—like a berry, fruit or vegetable—depending on the recipe. With the sour tang of a lemon, the tart moisture of an apple and the crisp grassiness of celery, it's a remarkable ingredient and a cook's dream.

These blush-colored stalks can be shaved, roasted, stewed or baked, but my favorite way to satisfy a rhubarb craving is in beverages. I've read that sailors of yore who didn't have access to citrus fruit were sometimes issued rhubarb to combat scurvy. That makes sense to me. I keep a bottle of rhubarb shrub (page 42) in my fridge at all times, and I have never had a hint of scurvy.

Despite its charms, rhubarb hasn't always been fit to eat. For centuries, it was confined to medicinal use, prized for its value as a purifying tonic. A big breakthrough came when Queen Victoria ascended to the British throne in 1837. Her coronation unleashed a rash of commemorative memorabilia and tributes, including a variety of sweeter, milder and more tender rhubarb that was easy to grow in kitchen gardens. The honorary Victoria Rhubarb yielded larger stalks in relation to the unusable leaves; it's now one of the most common varieties of rhubarb that grows, and we owe it a large debt for helping to move rhubarb from the medicine chest to the pie chest.

It's possible to buy rhubarb year-round, but local, seasonal rhubarb is a darling of spring and early summer. As a vigorous and persistent perennial, it pops up year after year, pushing the limits of its garden spot and stretching outward like a magenta sea anemone. As one of the first bumper crops to harvest each year, its consistent arrival has become part of our seasonal cooking rhythm, helping us make the mental transition into the produce-heavy summer months.

Rhubarb doesn't often inspire prose, much less poetry, but let me turn to the words of Groucho Marx: "Well, art is art, isn't it? Still, on the other hand, water is water! And east is east and west is west and if you take cranberries and stew them like applesauce they taste much more like prunes than rhubarb does. Now you tell me what you know."

—*Sheri Castle*

Recipes

Rhubarb Pancakes with Rhubarb Syrup

I credit a fortuitous cooking mistake for the amazing texture of these pancakes. I often fold whipped egg whites into pancake batter to make it light and airy, but when I was working on this recipe, I mistakenly added the egg white to the bowl without beating it. Not wanting to waste all the ingredients, I decided to cook a test pancake to see what would happen. It turns out that there's no need to whip the white; just adding it and the yolk separately is enough to yield impressively fluffy pancakes.

2 cups (8 ounces) finely diced fresh rhubarb

¼ cup firmly packed brown sugar, divided

3 tablespoons fresh lemon juice

1¼ cups all-purpose flour

1 teaspoon baking soda

1 teaspoon baking powder

¼ teaspoon kosher salt

1 cup well-shaken buttermilk

1 large egg, separated

2 tablespoons butter, melted and slightly cooled, plus more, softened, for the griddle and serving

Rhubarb Syrup (recipe follows), for serving

serves 4

In a bowl, stir together the rhubarb, 2 tablespoons of brown sugar and the lemon juice. Set aside for at least 10 minutes. In a large bowl, whisk together the remaining 2 tablespoons of sugar, the flour, baking soda, baking powder and salt.

In a small bowl, whisk together the buttermilk and egg yolk. Pour the buttermilk mixture into the flour mixture and stir until just combined. Stir in the egg white until thick, lumpy batter forms. Quickly stir in the melted butter. Fold in the rhubarb and any juices.

Heat a griddle or large skillet over medium-high heat and brush it with softened butter. Working in batches, pour ¼-cup measurements of batter onto the griddle, spacing them evenly. Using a rubber spatula or the back of a spoon, spread the batter for each pancake into a circle about 4 inches wide. Cook until browned on the bottom and bubbling on top, about 2½ minutes. Flip the pancakes and cook until the other side is browned, about 2 minutes longer. You'll need to adjust the heat up and down to keep the pancakes cooking evenly; you don't want the outsides to scorch while waiting for the insides to cook through. Serve the pancakes hot with plenty of soft butter and Rhubarb Syrup.

Rhubarb Syrup

It takes quite a bit of rhubarb to make full-flavored syrup. Bright-red stalks make the prettiest syrup, as they produce a beautiful pink color. The leftover strained pulp doesn't look like much, but I can't bring myself to throw it away (as it tastes delicious), so I stash it in a jar in the fridge and use it as a rustic compote to spread on toast and to stir into oatmeal or yogurt.

9 cups (about 2½ pounds) coarsely chopped fresh, bright-red rhubarb

3 cups sugar

makes 2 cups

In a large heavy saucepan, combine the rhubarb and sugar. Bring to a boil over medium-high heat, stirring until the sugar dissolves. Reduce the heat and simmer gently until the rhubarb is very soft and the liquid reduces to the consistency of pancake syrup or runny honey.

Strain the syrup through a fine-mesh sieve set over a bowl. Let the syrup drain for 30 minutes or so to extract every last drop, pressing very gently on the solids from time to time. Discard the solids or refrigerate, covered, for up to 2 weeks.

Transfer the syrup to a glass jar or bottle. Cover and refrigerate for up to 1 month.

Roasted Rhubarb & Rosy Custard Trifle

Roasting rhubarb with a little sugar creates glazed pieces that retain their shape and look attractive in this layered dessert. I use this same custard when I make banana pudding, but when I pair it with rhubarb, I can't resist adding a few drops of rosewater to the recipe. I adore the subtle fragrance of rosewater in sweet and fruity recipes, as one often finds in Middle Eastern desserts; however, not everyone appreciates floral flavors in food, so it's fine to replace the rosewater with more vanilla extract instead. When you don't have time to fool with a trifle, just spoon the warm rhubarb over ice cream.

For the roasted rhubarb:

2 tablespoons unsalted butter, at room temperature

6 tablespoons sugar, divided

1 pound fresh, brightred rhubarb, cut diagonally into 2-inch pieces (4 cups)

1 vanilla bean

For the custard and trifle:

¾ cup sugar

⅓ cup all-purpose flour

¼ teaspoon kosher salt

2 cups whole milk

4 large egg yolks

1 tablespoon unsalted butter

1 teaspoon rosewater

1 teaspoon pure vanilla extract

One 8-by-4-inch loaf plain or vanilla pound cake

serves 8

Make the rhubarb: Preheat the oven to 375°. Butter a 9-inch square baking dish and sprinkle with 2 tablespoons of sugar. Spread the rhubarb in a single layer in the prepared dish.

Split the vanilla bean lengthwise. Scrape the seeds into a small bowl, add the remaining 4 tablespoons of sugar and toss to mix. Sprinkle the vanilla sugar over the rhubarb. Tuck the vanilla bean pod in with the rhubarb.

Roast the rhubarb until it's tender when pierced with a knife, about 20 minutes. Discard the vanilla bean pod and set the rhubarb aside.

Make the custard: In a large heavy saucepan, whisk together the sugar, flour and salt. Whisking constantly, add the milk in a slow and steady stream. Whisk in the egg yolks. Cook over medium-high heat, stirring constantly with a rubber spatula, until the custard bubbles around the edges and thickly coats the spatula, 8 to 10 minutes. Remove the pan from the heat, add the butter and stir until it melts. Stir in the rosewater and vanilla.

To assemble the trifle, cut the pound cake into slices about ½ inch thick. Line the side and bottom of a 2½-quart trifle bowl or round baking dish with cake, breaking the slices into smaller pieces as needed. Spoon in one-third of the warm custard. Top with half of the rhubarb. Cover with a layer of the remaining cake. Spoon in one-third of the custard, followed by the rest of the rhubarb and any juices. Finish with the last third of the custard.

Serve the trifle warm or let cool to room temperature, cover and refrigerate until chilled.

Storing Rhubarb

Fresh rhubarb is quite perishable. Place whole stalks in a plastic bag to retain moisture and refrigerate for up to 5 days in the crisper drawer. Wash and trim the stalks just before using.

If your fresh rhubarb gets fatigued and a little droopy on the ride home from the market on a hot day, you can refresh it by standing the stalks upright in a jar or bowl that's filled with enough cool water to cover the bottom inch of the stalks; let stand for about an hour. Once the stalks have recovered, store them in the refrigerator.

Rhubarb Crumb Cake

A mug of hot coffee and a hunk of crumb cake with thick lumps of streusel are an exceptional way to start an ordinary day. This cake merits a plate, fork and a few minutes seated at the breakfast table in peaceful enjoyment. The small bits of rhubarb make this classic even more delicious without interfering with its essential crumb-cakeness. The cake is good the day it's baked, but I like it even better after an overnight rest—for both the cake and me. The next morning all I must do is brew coffee, eat, drink and repeat.

For the topping:

1 cup firmly packed dark brown sugar

½ cup granulated sugar

1 teaspoon ground cinnamon

1 teaspoon ground cardamom

½ teaspoon kosher salt

1 cup (2 sticks) unsalted butter, melted

2 cups all-purpose flour

For the cake:

2½ cups all-purpose flour

1 teaspoon baking soda

¾ teaspoon baking powder

½ teaspoon fine sea salt

¾ cup (1½ sticks) unsalted butter, at room temperature

1½ cups granulated sugar

2 large eggs, at room temperature

1½ cups sour cream

1 tablespoon pure vanilla extract

3 cups (12 ounces) finely diced rhubarb

serves 12

Make the topping: In a medium bowl, stir together the brown sugar, granulated sugar, cinnamon, cardamom and salt. Add the melted butter and stir until the mixture is smooth. Add the flour and stir until the mixture is crumbly with some moist clumps. Set aside until needed.

Make the cake: Preheat the oven to 350° and grease a 9-by-13-inch baking pan. Sift the flour, baking soda, baking powder and salt together into a large bowl.

In a separate large bowl, beat the butter with an electric mixer at high speed until smooth. With the mixer running, gradually add the sugar. Beat the mixture until light and fluffy, about 5 minutes. Add the eggs, one at a time, beating well after each addition. Add the sour cream and vanilla and beat just until smooth. Add the flour mixture in three equal additions, beating after each addition just until the batter is smooth. Fold in the rhubarb and scrape the batter into the prepared baking dish. Pinch off pieces of the topping into small clumps and drop evenly over the batter.

Bake the cake until a wooden pick inserted into it comes out clean, about 1 hour. The topping will be deep golden brown and crisp. Cool the cake on a wire rack until room temperature before serving.

Classic Rhubarb Jam

This recipe has been around forever, and I see no reason to change it. The jam is soft and spoonable, and the flavor is spot on. Rhubarb jam is an exercise in simplicity. In only 15 minutes, a few simple ingredients transform into a couple pints of greatness. For the best results, weigh the rhubarb and sugar to ensure the ratio is accurate. A benefit of making a small batch of jam is that you can enjoy (or share) it quickly enough that the jars can live in the refrigerator, which eliminates the need to seal them in a hot water bath. Classic recipes belong to no one, and to everyone.

---

1 fresh lemon

2½ pounds fresh or thawed rhubarb, cut crosswise into ½-inch-thick slices

1 pound sugar

¼ teaspoon kosher salt

makes 2 pints

Place a small glass or ceramic plate in the freezer to use to test the readiness of the jam.

Scrub and dry the lemon. Cut it in half and squeeze the juice into a small bowl. Discard the seeds and reserve the rinds.

In a large saucepan, stir together the rhubarb, sugar, salt and lemon rinds. Let the ingredients stand at room temperature for 1 hour, then bring to a boil over medium-high heat, stirring until the sugar dissolves. Cook at a low boil, stirring constantly and skimming away any foam that forms on top, until the bubbles reduce in size, the rhubarb rises to the top of the liquid and the jam falls in a sheet rather than in drips from a spoon, about 15 minutes.

Test the jam by spooning a little onto the chilled plate. If the dollop holds its shape without running, the jam is ready.

Remove the pan from the heat and stir in the lemon juice. Discard the rinds. Pour the jam into clean jars, let cool to room temperature, then cover and refrigerate for up to 3 months.

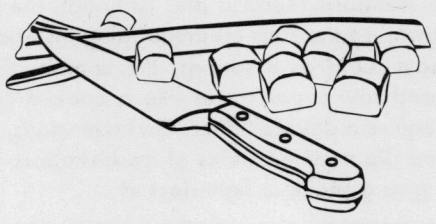

Fresh Versus Frozen

There's a notable difference between the texture of fresh and thawed rhubarb. Although both can play a delicious role in recipes, they're not always interchangeable. Crunchy fresh rhubarb is the obvious choice when it's to be served raw, and it's the best choice for recipes where pieces of cooked rhubarb must hold their shape. Rhubarb that's been frozen tastes fine, but freezing and thawing renders it soft and a little spongy, so it's best used in recipes where the rhubarb will be cooked until it breaks apart.

Many grocery stores sell frozen rhubarb, but to freeze your own, cut the stalks into 1-inch pieces, lay them flat on a parchment paper–lined baking pan and freeze until firm. Transfer to freezer bags, squeeze out the excess air and store in the freezer for up to a year. I freeze rhubarb in 1- or 2-cup portions—the amounts I use most often in recipes—to avoid thawing more rhubarb than I can use quickly.

Sour Cream Rhubarb Pie with Ginger-Pecan Streusel

The crumbly, crunchy streusel atop this pie puts it a notch or two above a standard rhubarb pie. Although the pie is plenty good on its own, try the sour cream topping instead of the usual whipped cream. Odd as it sounds, the combination of chilled sour cream and raw sugar tastes like a cooked custard sauce that should require a double boiler. On lazier days, I skip the pie altogether and dip trimmed stalks of fresh rhubarb into the sour cream topping as a snack or light dessert.

For the streusel:

¼ cup rolled oats

¼ cup firmly packed light brown sugar

2 tablespoons all-purpose flour

2 tablespoons unsalted butter, cut into cubes and softened

3 tablespoons chopped pecan pieces

1 tablespoon finely chopped candied ginger

For the filling:

3 cups (12 ounces) fresh rhubarb, cut into ½-inch cubes

One 9-inch deep-dish pie shell

1 cup granulated sugar

3 tablespoons instant or all-purpose flour

½ teaspoon kosher salt

1 teaspoon ground ginger

½ teaspoon freshly grated nutmeg

2 large eggs

1 cup sour cream

For the topping:

2 cups sour cream

½ cup demerara or other coarse raw sugar

Make the streusel: In a small bowl, stir together the oats, brown sugar and flour. Work in the butter with your fingertips until the mixture

is crumbly. Fold in the pecans and candied ginger. Refrigerate until chilled.

Make the filling: Preheat the oven to 400°. Place a baking sheet in the oven to get hot while the oven heats. Pour the rhubarb into the pie shell.

In a medium bowl, stir together the granulated sugar, flour, salt, ginger and nutmeg. In a small bowl, whisk together the eggs and sour cream, then add to the sugar mixture and stir to combine. Pour the filling over the rhubarb.

Place the pie on the hot baking sheet and bake for 10 minutes. Lower the temperature to 350° and bake for 30 minutes longer. Sprinkle the streusel topping over the pie and continue baking until the filling is puffed and set and the streusel browns, 20 to 25 minutes longer.

Let the pie cool to room temperature on a wire rack. (The filling will fall as it cools.)

Just before serving, make the topping: Stir together the sour cream and demerara sugar in a small bowl. Serve immediately, while the sugar is still crunchy, spooning a dollop of sour cream onto each slice of pie. (The sour cream mixture quickly loses its appealing crunch, so if you're not serving the entire pie at once, stir together only enough of the sour cream mixture needed at the time.)

Fish Tacos with Rhubarb-Pineapple Salsa

Tart, fresh rhubarb is the best choice for salsa because it holds its crisp texture even when mixed with acidic ingredients that can soften other fruits and vegetables. This recipe makes more salsa than is needed for the tacos, but that's no problem: Serve the rest with tortilla or sweet potato chips on the side. It keeps well in the refrigerator for a couple of days, although it gets juicier each day. When it gets too juicy to serve as salsa, pulse it in a blender to make fruity gazpacho.

This technique for cooking the fish yields crispy, crusty fish that isn't fried. Be sure to use fine cornmeal or corn flour because coarse stone-ground meal doesn't cook as quickly as the fish and the exterior will remain rough and gummy.

For the salsa:

2 cups (8 ounces) finely diced fresh rhubarb

1 cup finely diced fresh pineapple

½ cup finely diced red onion

Finely grated zest of 1 lime

Juice of 2 limes (about ¼ cup)

1 jalapeño, very finely chopped (remove the seeds for less heat)

½ teaspoon kosher salt

¼ cup pepper jelly or peach preserves

¼ cup coarsely chopped cilantro leaves

For the tacos:

1 pound skinless catfish or other thin, mild fish fillets, cut in half crosswise

Kosher salt and freshly ground black pepper

½ cup Wondra or all-purpose flour

¼ cup fine cornmeal or corn flour (masa)

1 tablespoon chile powder, or to taste

½ cup mayonnaise

3 tablespoons fresh lime juice

8 small flour tortillas, warmed, for serving

serves 4

Make the salsa: In a bowl, stir together the rhubarb, pineapple, onion, lime zest and juice, jalapeño, salt and jelly. Cover and refrigerate until needed. Just before serving, add the cilantro, stir well and check the seasoning.

Make the tacos: Position a rack in upper third of the oven and preheat the oven to 500°. Mist a rimmed baking sheet with vegetable oil spray or line it with nonstick aluminum foil.

Season the fish all over with salt and pepper. Whisk together the flour, cornmeal and chile powder in a shallow dish. Stir together the mayonnaise and lime juice in a small bowl. Using a brush, spread a thin layer of the mayonnaise mixture on both sides of the fish, then coat with the flour mixture, shaking off any excess. Arrange the fish in a single layer on the prepared baking sheet.

Bake until the crust is crisp and golden and the fish is cooked through, about 10 minutes. Serve immediately in warm tortillas with the salsa.

Pulled Chicken Sandwiches with Rhubarb Barbecue Sauce

Rhubarb adds body, flavor and intrigue to barbecue sauce. It's noticeable and complex, yet hard to identify. This sauce is a great way to both start a conversation and finish a chicken sandwich.

Grilled chicken with barbecue sauce usually sounds better than it turns out, or at least that was the case when I was a kid. My family would drench raw chicken in sweet bottled sauce and sling it over flaming charcoal soaked in lighter fluid. The sauce would blacken and smolder long before the chicken was done. I learned that the best way for a grilling duffer like me to achieve best results is to coat cooked chicken with sauce and pile it onto buttered and toasted buns.

---

3 to 4 cups coarsely shredded grilled chicken

1½ to 2 cups Rhubarb Barbecue Sauce (recipe follows)

6 sandwich buns

2 tablespoons unsalted butter, softened

12 dill pickle slices

Place the chicken in a medium saucepan. Add enough sauce to generously coat and moisten the chicken, but not so much that the mixture turns soupy. Cook gently over medium heat until the chicken and sauce are warmed through, about 5 minutes.

Meanwhile, butter the cut sides of the buns. In a hot skillet, cook the buns, buttered-side down, until browned and toasted, about 3 minutes.

Divide the chicken among the buns and top each sandwich with two pickle slices. Serve warm.

Rhubarb Barbecue Sauce

This recipe yields more sauce than you'll need for six sandwiches, but it keeps well and you can use it as you would any barbecue sauce. The ground chipotle chile gives it a real kick, but for a meeker sauce, replace some or all of the chipotle with smoked paprika. Because the sauce is pureed, this is a great way to use frozen rhubarb.

---

3 cups (12 ounces) fresh or thawed diced rhubarb

½ cup Rhubarb Ketchup (page 30)

¼ cup honey

¼ cup packed light brown sugar

2 tablespoons Creole mustard or whole-grain Dijon mustard

½ cup Tart Rhubarb Vinegar (page 41) or unfiltered apple cider vinegar

1 teaspoon kosher salt

¾ teaspoon coarsely ground black pepper

1 teaspoon ground chipotle chile powder

½ teaspoon garlic powder

1 cup tart cherry juice

makes 4 cups

In a large saucepan, combine all of the ingredients and bring to a boil over medium-high heat. Reduce the heat and simmer until the rhubarb is tender, about 15 minutes.

Puree in a blender until smooth, or puree directly in the pan with an immersion blender.

Use the sauce while it's still warm, or transfer it to a jar and let cool to room temperature, then cover and refrigerate for up to 2 weeks.

Smothered Chicken with Rhubarb Gravy

This variation of classic Southern smothered chicken has the tangy addition of rhubarb mixed in with the caramelized onions. The surprise addition of crushed gingersnaps is a nod to the Moravian cooking found in the historic Old Salem community in Winston-Salem, North Carolina. The same technique can be found in German sauerbraten gravy. Serve this over mashed russet or sweet potatoes to soak up every comforting drop.

- 3 tablespoons extra-virgin olive oil, divided
- 5 tablespoons unsalted butter, divided
- 2 large onions, halved lengthwise and thinly sliced
- Kosher salt
- 5 cups (1¼ pounds) fresh rhubarb, cut on the diagonal into 1-inch slices
- 1½ cups Wondra or all-purpose flour
- 1 teaspoon freshly ground black pepper
- 3 pounds skinless, boneless chicken thighs
- 1½ cups chicken stock
- 1½ cups whole milk
- ½ cup bourbon or brandy
- ⅓ cup whole-grain Dijon mustard
- 6 tablespoons crushed gingersnap cookies
- 2 tablespoons chopped thyme leaves, for garnish

serves 8

In a large heavy (preferably cast-iron) skillet, heat 1 tablespoon of oil and 1 tablespoon of butter over medium-high heat. Stir in the onions and a large pinch of salt. Cover and cook until the onions soften, about 15 minutes. Uncover and continue cooking, stirring often, until the onions are very soft and golden, about 15 minutes longer. Add the rhubarb and cook until barely tender, about 5 minutes. Scrape the mixture into a bowl and set aside. Wipe out the skillet.

Stir together the flour, 1 tablespoon of salt and the pepper on a plate. Lightly and evenly coat the chicken in the flour mixture, shaking off the excess. Place the chicken on a plate in a single layer to dry a little while the skillet gets hot. Reserve ¼ cup of the seasoned flour.

Heat 2 tablespoons of oil and 2 tablespoons of butter in the skillet over medium-high heat. When the butter stops foaming, add the chicken, leaving space between the pieces so they'll brown instead of steam (work in batches, if necessary). Cook the chicken undisturbed until it's richly browned on the bottom and releases easily from the skillet, about 3 minutes. Turn the chicken over and brown the other side, adjusting the heat as needed to prevent any bits of flour that float into the fat from burning. Transfer the browned chicken to a clean plate and set aside.

Combine the chicken stock and milk in a saucepan and warm over low heat (do not simmer). Carefully add the bourbon to the skillet and, using a wooden spoon, scrape up the browned bits from the bottom of the pan. When the liquid has nearly cooked away, add the remaining 2 tablespoons of butter. Sprinkle the reserved seasoned flour over the pan drippings and whisk until smooth. Cook, whisking, for 2 minutes.

Whisk in the chicken stock-milk mixture and cook, stirring with a rubber spatula, until the gravy is thick enough to coat the back of the spatula, about 5 minutes. Stir in the mustard, gingersnaps and reserved onions and rhubarb. Cook until the gravy gently bubbles.

Return the chicken to the pan and cook until the juices run clear when the thighs are pierced with the tip of a knife, about 5 minutes. Sprinkle with the thyme and serve hot.

Rhubarb & Root Vegetable Tagine with Pistachio Couscous

I learned to make tagine, a North African style of stew, from a Moroccan friend. His featured meat and was cooked in a beautiful clay vessel, but I've come up with my own version: a colorful vegetable tagine that's prepared in a Dutch oven. Even without the meat, this dish has plenty of richness; the addition of acerbic rhubarb helps to keep it in check. I like to top each serving with a drizzle of tangy pomegranate molasses. If you like a little fiery heat, top the stew with a dab of *harissa* chile paste in addition to the molasses. You can find bottles of pomegranate molasses and tubes, cans or jars of *harissa* in Middle Eastern markets and the international section of well-stocked grocery stores.

serves 6 to 8

For the tagine:

5 tablespoons clarified butter (ghee) or vegetable oil, divided

1 large onion, halved lengthwise and thinly sliced

1 teaspoon garam masala

1 teaspoon ground cinnamon

¼ teaspoon cayenne pepper

1 teaspoon kosher salt, plus more to taste

½ teaspoon freshly ground black pepper

1 rutabaga (12 ounces), peeled and cut into bite-size chunks

2 small sweet potatoes (8 ounces), peeled and cut into bite-size chunks

2 medium carrots (4 ounces), peeled and cut into bite-size chunks

2 medium parsnips (4 ounces), peeled and cut into bite-size chunks

2 large red and/or yellow bell peppers, cored and cut into bite-size chunks

8 ounces fresh rhubarb, cut into bite-size chunks

1 cup chicken or vegetable stock

One 14.5-ounce can diced tomatoes

One 14.5-ounce can chickpeas, drained and rinsed

½ cup currants or raisins

Pomegranate molasses, for serving

Harissa paste, for serving

For the pistachio couscous:

3 cups chicken or vegetable stock	1 teaspoon kosher salt
1 tablespoon extra-virgin olive oil	1½ cups uncooked couscous
	½ cup shelled salted whole pistachios

Make the tagine: Add 2 tablespoons of clarified butter to a Dutch oven and place over medium heat. When the butter is warm, add the onion, cover and cook until softened, about 8 minutes, stirring occasionally. Stir in the garam masala, cinnamon, cayenne, salt and pepper and cook for 2 minutes, stirring constantly. Transfer the onion mixture to a large bowl and set aside.

Add another 2 tablespoons of clarified butter to the Dutch oven and heat over medium heat. Add the rutabaga, sweet potato, carrots and parsnips and stir to coat. Cover and cook until the vegetables are crisp-tender, about 12 minutes, stirring occasionally to make sure the spices don't scorch (add a splash of water if needed). Using a slotted spoon, transfer the vegetables to the bowl of onions.

Heat the remaining tablespoon of clarified butter in the Dutch oven over medium heat. Stir in the peppers and rhubarb; cover and cook, stirring occasionally, until crisp-tender, about 5 minutes.

Return the onion-vegetable mixture to the pot. Stir in the stock and tomatoes and simmer until the vegetables are just tender, about 10 minutes. Stir in the chickpeas and currants and heat through. Taste the broth and adjust the seasoning; the stew should be bold and bright. Keep the tagine warm over low heat.

Meanwhile, make the couscous: In a large saucepan, bring the stock, oil and salt to a boil. Stir in the couscous. Remove the pan from the heat, cover and let stand until the couscous absorbs the liquid, 7 to 10 minutes. Fluff the couscous with a fork and stir in the pistachios. Spoon the couscous into shallow bowls and top with ladles of the tagine. Finish with a generous drizzle of pomegranate molasses and/or harissa and serve.

Pecan-Crusted Salmon with Crisp Rhubarb & Apple Slaw

Eating raw rhubarb is a first for many people, even those who love it cooked. It's crunchy, juicy, tart and astringent, rather like a sour apple. The first bite can be shocking, the second bite is intriguing and, by the third bite, you're hooked. I can't get enough of the stuff, and I often munch on stalks as others might snack on carrots or celery. The crunch and invigorating taste of raw rhubarb make it a great choice for slaw to accompany rich fish like wild salmon. Shaving short lengths of red rhubarb into ribbons showcases its color and crispness—and makes it easy to serve and eat. (It's also practical: Rhubarb does not grate well.) It's crucial to use soft, fresh breadcrumbs here. I make them from slices of sandwich bread or dinner rolls.

For the salmon:

Six 6-ounce center-cut wild salmon fillets, with skin

1 teaspoon kosher salt

½ teaspoon freshly ground black pepper

¼ cup (½ stick) unsalted butter, melted

¼ cup whole-grain Dijon mustard

¼ cup honey

1 cup soft, fresh breadcrumbs

½ cup finely chopped pecans

For the slaw:

3 tablespoons extra-virgin olive oil

3 tablespoons honey

3 tablespoons fresh lemon juice

1 teaspoon whole-grain Dijon mustard

Kosher salt and freshly ground black pepper

2 cups shredded Savoy cabbage

1 small red onion, halved lengthwise and thinly sliced

6 ounces medium-size fresh rhubarb stalks

1 small Honeycrisp apple

2 tablespoons chervil, parsley or beet microgreens

serves 6

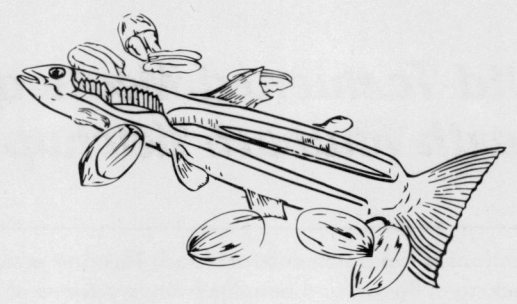

Make the salmon: Preheat the oven to 350° and line a rimmed baking sheet with foil.

Place the salmon fillets, skin side down, on the foil and season with salt and pepper. In a small bowl, stir together the butter, mustard and honey. Coat the tops of the fillets with the mustard mixture.

Mix the breadcrumbs and pecans in a small bowl. Top each fillet with the breadcrumb mixture, pressing lightly to help it adhere. Roast the salmon until it's barely opaque in the center, 13 to 18 minutes.

Meanwhile, make the slaw: Whisk together the oil, honey, lemon juice and mustard in a large bowl. Season generously with salt and pepper.

Add the cabbage and onion to the bowl. Cut the rhubarb into 3-inch lengths. Use a mandoline or vegetable peeler to shave each piece into thin ribbons and add them to the bowl. Quarter the apple and remove the core. Use a mandoline or vegetable peeler to shave each piece into thin ribbons and add them to the bowl. Toss to coat with the dressing and let stand for 5 minutes. Stir and check the seasoning just before serving.

To serve, divide the slaw among six plates. Run a thin metal spatula between the salmon fillets and skin and lift the fillets, leaving the skin on the foil. Top the slaw on each plate with a warm salmon fillet, sprinkle with chervil and serve at once.

Old-Fashioned Meatloaf with Rhubarb Ketchup

Good meatloaf is top-notch comfort food. This one is restrained, but not lacking in flavor, and benefits from two forms of rhubarb. First, fresh rhubarb stands in for celery in the mirepoix, making this recipe a great way to use up any rhubarb stalks that are too green, slender and tart to use otherwise. The Rhubarb Ketchup provides a second wave of rhubarb's punchiness. Ketchup, of any sort, should be a condiment for meatloaf, not a cloaking device.

I prefer thick, deeply browned crust on meatloaf, so I bake this in a cast-iron skillet, but it's fine to bake it in a loaf pan or shape the mixture into a loaf on a rimmed baking sheet. This meatloaf is more crumbly than sliceable, so if you want to make sandwiches with any leftovers, reheat scoops in a skillet and pile the meat onto a bun, as you would a sloppy Joe.

½ cup soft, fresh breadcrumbs

3 tablespoons whole milk

1 tablespoon unsalted butter

1 cup finely chopped onion

¾ cup finely chopped fresh rhubarb

½ cup finely chopped carrot

2 teaspoons kosher salt

½ teaspoon freshly ground black pepper

1 tablespoon finely chopped garlic

12 ounces lean ground beef

6 ounces ground pork

2 smoky bacon slices, finely chopped

2 teaspoons Worcestershire sauce

2 teaspoons soy sauce

⅓ cup Rhubarb Ketchup, plus more for serving (page 31)

1 large egg, beaten

¼ cup finely chopped flat-leaf parsley

Serves 4 to 6

Preheat the oven to 350°.

In a bowl, stir together the breadcrumbs and milk; set aside until needed.

In a 9- or 10-inch cast-iron skillet, melt the butter over medium-high heat. Add the onion, rhubarb, carrot, salt and pepper and cook until tender, stirring occasionally, about 5 minutes. Add the garlic and cook for 1 minute longer. Pour the mixture into a large bowl and let cool for 5 minutes.

Add the beef, pork, bacon, Worcestershire, soy sauce, ketchup, egg, parsley and the breadcrumb mixture to the bowl. Using your hands, mix until just combined. Press the meatloaf mixture into the skillet. Bake until an instant-read thermometer inserted into the center of the meat registers 155°, 45 to 60 minutes, depending on the thickness of the loaf. Let the meatloaf cool for 15 minutes before serving with more Rhubarb Ketchup on the side.

Rhubarb Ketchup

This smooth, piquant sauce reminds us that tomatoes didn't always have the monopoly on ketchup. The word ketchup historically referred to a host of highly spiced fermented or cooked sauces offered at the table. They could be made from a number of ingredients, such as walnuts, oysters, elderberries or mushrooms. Because of rhubarb's affinity for pungent spices, it makes excellent ketchup.

You can use Rhubarb Ketchup as an ingredient, a dipping sauce, or whenever and whenever you use regular ketchup. To transform this ketchup into chutney, skip the pureeing step.

- 4 cups (1 pound) chopped fresh or thawed rhubarb
- 1 cup chopped red onion
- ¼ cup golden raisins
- ½ cup sugar
- ½ cup Rhubarb Vinegar (page 41) or unfiltered apple cider vinegar
- Finely grated zest and juice of 1 orange
- 1 tablespoon finely grated fresh ginger
- ½ teaspoon ground cinnamon
- ½ teaspoon whole yellow mustard seed
- ½ teaspoon whole coriander seed
- ½ teaspoon kosher salt
- ¼ teaspoon ground cayenne pepper
- ⅛ teaspoon ground cloves
- 2 tablespoons ruby port wine

makes 3 cups

In a large saucepan, stir together all of the ingredients except the port wine. Bring to a boil over medium-high heat. Remove the pan from the heat, stir well, cover and let stand for 1 hour.

Return the mixture to a boil, then reduce the heat to medium and simmer until the rhubarb is tender and the cooking liquid coats the back of a wooden spoon, about 10 minutes. Remove the pan from the heat, stir in the port wine and let cool to room temperature.

Puree in a blender or directly in the pot with an immersion blender. Transfer the ketchup to a glass jar, cover tightly and refrigerate until chilled. Store covered and refrigerated for up to a month.

Pork Chops with Rhubarb Pan Dressing

Apples and pork might be a classic dinner duo, but no apple can hold a candle to rhubarb in this dish. Even though rhubarb mellows when it's cooked, it remains interesting and flavorful. The delicious juices from the roasting pork and rhubarb mingle with the aromatic spices to flavor the bread, making the dressing a little crisp and sticky on the edges and tender in the center. This homey, filling one-dish dinner is ready to serve in less than an hour.

---

2 cups (8 ounces) fresh rhubarb, cut into bite-size pieces

2 cups bite-size pieces of country-style bread

½ cup packed light brown sugar

½ teaspoon ground cinnamon

¼ teaspoon ground allspice

¼ teaspoon dry mustard

2 teaspoons chopped rosemary

1 teaspoon kosher salt, divided

½ teaspoon freshly ground black pepper, divided

4 bone-in pork loin chops (each about 9 ounces)

1 tablespoon vegetable oil

1 tablespoon unsalted butter

serves 4

Preheat the oven to 350°.

In a large bowl, stir together the rhubarb, bread, sugar, cinnamon, allspice, mustard, rosemary, ½ teaspoon of salt and ¼ teaspoon of pepper.

Season the pork chops with the remaining ½ teaspoon of salt and ¼ teaspoon of pepper. In a large skillet (preferably cast-iron), heat the oil and butter over medium-high heat. Add the pork chops and cook, undisturbed, until browned on the bottom, about 3 minutes. (When they're sufficiently browned, they'll release from the pan easily.) Turn the chops over and brown the other side.

Spoon the rhubarb mixture around the chops. (If your skillet won't hold the chops and all the dressing, transfer them to a buttered shallow baking dish.)

Cover the skillet tightly with foil and transfer to the oven; bake for 20 minutes. Uncover and continue baking until an instant-read thermometer inserted into the center of a chop registers 145°, about 10 minutes longer. Let the chops rest for 5 minutes before serving warm.

Duck à la Rouge

I studied French for a few years, which led to some curiosity about classic French recipes. My beloved grandmother delighted in my cooking and was always willing to sample my experiments and discoveries, especially items I brought home after I moved away to college. One semester, I bought a whole frozen duck at a Chapel Hill grocery store, something I'd never find in my hometown of Boone, North Carolina. I dutifully followed a recipe for duck à l'orange with high hopes. Good lord, it was awful. The sauce was passable, but that freezer-burned duck proved hopeless. However, it was not so awful that I gave up on duck—or sauces. Over time, I figured out that fresh duck breasts are key, and that fruity cooked rhubarb and juniper berries are fitting upgrades for the sauce.

Most recipes for duck breasts call for searing them in a screaming hot skillet, but I prefer cooking them over moderate heat so that the fat renders slowly and the skin crisps beautifully. With this recipe, the judicious use of heat is key so that the spices don't burn. The duck skin will be deeply browned, on the edge of charred, but it shouldn't taste acrid. Be sure your spices are fresh and deeply fragrant; otherwise you're adding little more than dust to the duck.

For the duck:

4 teaspoons juniper berries

½ teaspoon ground cinnamon

½ teaspoon ground mace

½ teaspoon dry mustard

½ teaspoon ground ginger

¼ teaspoon ground allspice

2 teaspoons kosher salt

½ teaspoon freshly ground black pepper

2 fresh magret duck breasts (about 1 pound each)

For the sauce:

¼ cup sugar

2 tablespoons Rhubarb Vinegar (page 41) or sherry vinegar

1½ cups freshly squeezed orange juice

2 tablespoons finely chopped shallot

1½ cups duck or chicken stock

2 cups (8 ounces) fresh rhubarb, cut on the diagonal into ½-inch slices

1 orange

For the cabbage:

½ small red cabbage head, cored and shredded (about 6 cups)

2 teaspoons brown sugar

serves 4

Make the duck: Place the juniper berries in a small skillet. Cook over medium-high heat, swirling the pan gently, until the berries are shiny, about 90 seconds. Remove the pan from the heat and add the cinnamon, mace, mustard, ginger and allspice. Let stand until the spices release their aromas, about 30 seconds. Pour the spices into a spice grinder or mortar and pestle; add the salt and pepper, and pulse or pulverize until finely ground.

Pat the duck breasts dry. Using a sharp knife, score the thick fat cap (without cutting into the meat) in a crosshatch pattern to form 1-inch diamonds. Sprinkle 1 teaspoon of the spice blend evenly over both sides of each duck breast. Set aside the remaining spice blend to use in the cabbage. Preheat the oven to 400° and let the duck breasts stand at room temperature while you make the sauce, at least 30 minutes.

Make the sauce: Pour the sugar and 2 tablespoons of water into a medium heavy saucepan. Cook over medium heat, stirring occasionally, until the sugar dissolves and the mixture turns the color of dark amber, about

6 minutes. Add the vinegar; the mixture will hiss and sizzle vigorously. Swirl the pan until the mixture is completely combined. Add the orange juice and shallot and simmer until the liquid reduces to about ½ cup, about 15 minutes. Add the stock and simmer for 20 minutes. Stir in the rhubarb and cook until barely tender, about 10 minutes. Keep warm over very low heat.

Make the duck: Arrange the duck, skin side down, in a large cast-iron skillet. Place the skillet over medium-low heat and cook the duck, undisturbed, until the skin is deeply browned and crisp and much of the fat has rendered, about 15 minutes. (Lower the heat if you see black specks of spice floating in the fat.) Transfer the duck breasts to a plate and pour the rendered fat into a container. Return the breasts to the skillet, skin side up. Place the skillet in the oven to roast until the meat is done to your liking, about 10 minutes for rare and 13 minutes for medium-rare. Transfer the breasts to a plate to rest while the cabbage cooks.

Make the cabbage: Return the skillet (without cleaning) to the stovetop (keeping in mind that the handle will be very hot from having been in the oven). Add the cabbage and toss to coat in the residual duck fat. Sprinkle with 2 teaspoons of the reserved spice blend and the sugar. Cook over medium-high heat, tossing occasionally with tongs, until lightly wilted, about 7 minutes. Season to taste with salt and pepper.

Cut the orange into supremes: Cut off the tip and tail ends of the fruit. Set it down on a flat work surface and remove the peel and pith by cutting strips off the fruit vertically, following the contour of the fruit. Once all of the peel has been removed, cut out the segments of orange between each membrane. Discard the leftover membrane and stir the orange supremes into the sauce. Cut the duck into ½-inch-thick slices. Divide the cabbage among four plates, top each with a serving of duck and sauce and serve at once.

Rhubarb & Tomato Dumplings

Fluffy, biscuit-like dumplings are the feather beds of Southern comfort food. Chicken dumplings are the most famous, but Southerners are also skilled at adding dumplings to pots of bubbling fruit or vegetable stews. I adore old-fashioned tomato dumplings made by topping chunky stewed tomatoes with dollops of biscuit dough. One day I had a flash of inspired curiosity about whether ripe tomatoes and rhubarb would work well together, so the next time I made dumplings, I added chunks of rhubarb, and a new family favorite was born. The dish is filling enough to serve as a meatless entrée, but it also makes a nice side to a beef or pork roast.

For the stew:

4 tablespoons (½ stick) unsalted butter

1 cup chopped onion

2 teaspoons dried Italian herb blend or dried basil

1 bay leaf

1½ teaspoons kosher salt, plus more to taste

½ teaspoon freshly ground black pepper, plus more to taste

One 28-ounce can whole tomatoes, coarsely chopped, with their juices

3 cups (12 ounces) diced fresh or thawed rhubarb

¼ cup firmly packed light brown sugar

¼ cup sherry vinegar

For the dumplings:

1 cup all-purpose flour

1½ teaspoons baking powder

½ teaspoon kosher salt

1 tablespoon unsalted butter, cut into cubes and chilled

1 large egg, lightly beaten

½ cup whole milk

2 tablespoons finely chopped basil

Make the stew: In a large skillet or wide saucepan, melt the butter over medium-high heat. Add the onion, herb blend, bay leaf, salt and pepper; cook, stirring occasionally, until the onion is tender, about 5 minutes. Stir in the tomatoes, rhubarb, sugar and vinegar. Bring the mixture to a boil over high heat, then reduce to a simmer and cook gently until the rhubarb is tender but not falling apart, about 10 minutes.

Meanwhile, make the dumplings: In a medium bowl, whisk together the flour, baking powder and salt. Work in the chilled butter with a pastry blender or your fingertips until the mixture is crumbly. Make a well in the center and add the egg, milk and basil. Stir only until thick, soft, slightly sticky dough forms.

Using a small ice cream scoop or two spoons, drop rounded tablespoonsful of dough evenly over the surface of the bubbling stew. Cover the pan and cook until a toothpick inserted into a dumpling comes out clean, about 15 minutes. If the dumplings are still a bit wet on top, baste them with a little of the stew's liquid. Discard the bay leaf. Ladle the stew and dumplings into bowls and serve at once.

Rhubarb & Chard Gratin

I rely on the versatility of gratins. Take almost any vegetable, bathe it in creamy cheese sauce, crown it with buttered crumbs, and you have a winner. Imagine my disappointment when my first attempt at rhubarb gratin was less than stellar. It needed greenery, but rhubarb leaves are inedible, so I went to the grocery store to scout out surrogate leaves. Chard won, especially pretty ruby chard with red stems that match rhubarb stalks so closely in color that one cannot help but think they're cousins. (They aren't, by the way. Chard is a rootless beet, and rhubarb is a member of the buckwheat family.) I'll settle for calling them kindred spirits.

- 1 cup fresh white breadcrumbs
- ½ cup (2 ounces) freshly grated Parmesan cheese
- 6 tablespoons unsalted butter, divided, plus more for the pan
- 2 tablespoons Wondra or all-purpose flour
- 1½ cups whole milk, warmed
- ½ cup (2 ounces) freshly grated Gruyère cheese
- 1 teaspoon kosher salt
- ½ teaspoon dry mustard
- ¼ teaspoon freshly grated nutmeg
- ¼ teaspoon ground cayenne pepper
- 1 medium onion, finely chopped
- 1½ pounds ruby chard, stems cut into 1-inch pieces and leaves shredded
- 3 cups (12 ounces) fresh rhubarb, cut crosswise into 1-inch pieces
- 3 large garlic cloves, finely chopped

serves 8

Preheat the oven to 400° and generously butter a 2½-quart gratin or shallow baking dish. In a small bowl, stir together the breadcrumbs and Parmesan. Melt 2 tablespoons of butter, and drizzle over the breadcrumb mixture, tossing to coat.

In a medium saucepan, melt 2 tablespoons of the butter over medium-high heat. Whisk in the flour and cook for 2 minutes, whisking constantly. Whisk in the warm milk and cook, stirring with a heatproof rubber spatula, until the sauce thickens enough to coat the back of the spatula, about 3 minutes. Remove the pan from the heat and stir in the Gruyère, salt, mustard, nutmeg and cayenne. Set aside until needed, stirring occasionally to prevent a skin from forming.

In a large skillet over medium-high heat, melt the remaining 2 tablespoons of butter. Add the onion and cook until crisp-tender, stirring often, about 5 minutes. Add the chard stems, rhubarb and garlic; cook until the vegetables are tender, about 5 minutes longer. Add the chard leaves one large handful at a time, tossing with tongs until they lightly wilt before adding more. Cook until all the leaves have wilted, about 2 minutes. Pour in the cream sauce and stir to coat. Season to taste with salt and pepper. Pour the mixture into the prepared baking dish.

Sprinkle the breadcrumb mixture over the gratin and bake until the topping is golden brown and the rhubarb mixture is bubbling, about 20 minutes. Let the gratin stand for 10 minutes before serving warm.

Herbed Rhubarb Lemonade

Good lemonade makes people smile. Great rhubarb lemonade makes people smile and say nice things about you.

The key to this great lemonade is to double down on tartness with both lemon and rhubarb, and then balance it with just enough sugar to make it pleasing. A handful of fragrant herbs further distinguishes this pink lemonade for grown-ups.

---

5 cups (1¼ pounds) chopped fresh rhubarb, plus a few slender stalks for garnish

1 cup sugar, preferably unrefined sugar

Zest of 1 lemon, cut into wide strips with a vegetable peeler

½ cup lightly packed fresh mint, lemon verbena or basil leaves (or a mixture)

1 cup freshly squeezed Meyer lemon juice

2 cups sparkling water

Sprigs of mint, basil or lemon verbena, for garnish

Lemon slices, for garnish

serves 6

In a large saucepan over medium-high heat, bring 4 cups of water, the rhubarb and sugar to a boil, stirring until the sugar dissolves. Reduce the heat and simmer for 20 minutes. Remove the pan from the heat and stir in the lemon zest and herb leaves. Cover and let stand until cool. Strain the liquid into a large glass jar or pitcher and discard the solids.

Stir in the lemon juice and sparkling water. Cover and refrigerate until chilled. Serve the lemonade over ice, garnished with the herb sprigs, lemon slices and a length of rhubarb.

Tart Rhubarb Vinegar

This infused vinegar tastes like what you'd expect: acidic, rhubarby and pucker inducing. Use it in recipes (including several in this book) as you would other bold vinegars. The method couldn't be easier. Just keep in mind: The redder the rhubarb, the pinker the finished vinegar.

---

2 cups (8 ounces) thinly sliced rhubarb

1 to 1½ cups white distilled vinegar

Place the rhubarb in a pint jar. Add enough vinegar to cover the rhubarb.

Cover the jar and let it stand in a cool, dark place for at least 1 week. When the vinegar is as strongly flavored as you like, strain the contents of the jar through a fine-mesh sieve and discard the solids. Refrigerate the vinegar for up to 3 months.

Rhubarb Shrub (Shrubarb!)

This is my favorite recipe in this book. Making shrub concentrates the flavor of the rhubarb and bolsters it with both sweetness and acidity, so this might be the rhubarbiest concoction ever. Use the reddest fresh rhubarb you can find so that the shrub turns out rosy and gorgeous.

Shrubs—syrups made from fruit, sugar and vinegar—are making a comeback. The name comes from *sharbah*, the Arabic word for a drink. (The word "syrup" also comes from *sharbah*.) Shrubs beg to be used in beverages. Stir some into fizzy water or sparkling wine. Use it in creative cocktails. Sip it straight as a virgin aperitif or digestif. Beyond beverages, Rhubarb Shrub sits pretty in such recipes as a frosty granita and in place of vinegar in vinaigrettes, as in the recipes on the opposite page.

---

2 pounds (8 cups) bright-red fresh rhubarb, thinly sliced

1 cup white wine vinegar

1 cup sugar

makes 3 cups

In a medium saucepan, stir together the rhubarb, vinegar and sugar. Bring to a boil over medium-high heat, stirring until the sugar dissolves. Reduce the heat and simmer gently until the liquid is syrupy, about 15 minutes, stirring occasionally.

Strain the mixture through a fine-mesh sieve lined with a large paper coffee filter or cheesecloth and set over a bowl. Let the mixture stand undisturbed for an hour. Don't press on the solids or you run the risk of making the vinegar cloudy. Discard the solids and pour the vinegar into a glass jar or bottle, cover and refrigerate for up to 3 months.

Rhubarb Shrub Granita

Shrub makes tart, bracing granita—a frozen delight that doesn't require an ice cream maker. For fancier affairs, I garnish each serving with a few drops of exquisite aged balsamic vinegar. To serve on lazy warm evenings out on the porch when my backyard is ablaze with lightning bugs, I make playful slushies by scooping the granita into glasses and drizzling with more shrub.

3 cups Rhubarb Shrub

Stir together the shrub and 1 cup of cold water in a 9-by-13-inch baking dish. Cover with plastic wrap and place in the freezer.

Every 30 minutes or so, use a fork to rake up the slush and spread it around evenly. After about 3 hours, the granita will be consistently slushy with large granular crystals. Scrape the granita into serving bowls or glasses and serve ice cold.

Rhubarb Shrub Vinaigrette

This vinaigrette is delicious atop any fruit or simple green salad that benefits from a touch of sweetness. To use Rhubarb Shrub in your favorite vinaigrette, use it in place of the vinegar.

¼ cup Rhubarb Shrub

½ teaspoon Dijon mustard

2 teaspoons finely chopped shallot

5 tablespoons grapeseed oil

1 tablespoon finely chopped basil or mint

Kosher salt and freshly ground black pepper

In a small bowl, whisk together the shrub, mustard, and shallot. Whisking constantly, add the oil in a slow, steady stream. Whisk in the basil or mint. Season to taste with salt and pepper.

Thank You!

I'd like to thank Kaitlyn Goalen and Nick Fauchald for giving me the opportunity to be part of the Short Stack crew, the coolest writing gig ever. Thank you to rhubarb for waving its ruby red freak flag in the garden. Thanks to the benevolent forces that let me be Lily's mama and to live with a cadre of fur angels: Domino, Thimble and Wren. And with eternal gratitude I thank my Mama Madge for craving rhubarb and for making sure I understood love and good cooking.

—*Sheri Castle*

Share your Short Stack cooking experiences with us
(or just keep in touch) via:

 #shortstackeds

 facebook.com/shortstackeditions

 @shortstackeds

 hello@shortstackeditions.com

Colophon

This edition of Short Stack was printed by Stephen Gould Corp. in Richmond, Virginia on Neenah Astrobrights Pulsar Pink (interior) and Neenah Oxford White (cover) paper. The main text of the book is set in Futura and Jensen Pro, and the headlines are set in Lobster.

Available now at ShortStackEditions.com:

Vol. 1 | Eggs, by Ian Knauer

Vol. 2 | Tomatoes, by Soa Davies

Vol. 3 | Strawberries, by Susan Spungen

Vol. 4 | Buttermilk, by Angie Mosier

Vol. 5 | Grits, by Virginia Willis

Vol. 6 | Sweet Potatoes, by Scott Hocker

Vol. 7 | Broccoli, by Tyler Kord

Vol. 8 | Honey, by Rebekah Peppler

Vol. 9 | Plums, by Martha Holmberg

Vol. 10 | Corn, by Jessica Battilana

Vol. 11 | Apples, by Andrea Albin

Vol. 12 | Brown Sugar, by Libbie Summers

Vol. 13 | Lemons, by Alison Roman

Vol. 14 | Prosciutto di Parma, by Sara Jenkins

Vol. 15 | Summer Squash, by Sarah Baird

Vol. 16 | Peaches, by Beth Lipton

Vol. 17 | Chickpeas, by Victoria Granof

Vol. 18 | Chocolate, by Susie Heller

Vol. 19 | Maple Syrup, by Casey Elsass

Vol. 20 | Rhubarb, by Sheri Castle

Vol. 21 | Cherries, by Stacy Adimando

Vol. 22 | Eggplant, by Raquel Pelzel

Vol. 23 | Tahini, by Adeena Sussman

Vol. 24 | Ginger, by Mindy Fox

Vol. 25 | Avocados, by Katie Quinn

Vol. 26 | Peanuts, by Steven Satterfield

Vol. 27 | Coconut, by Ben Mims

Vol. 28 | Cucumbers, by Dawn Perry

Vol. 29 | Pears, by Andrea Slonecker